DEBUTS & FAREWELLS

DEBUTS & FAREWELLS

A Two-Decade Photographic Chronicle of the Metropolitan Opera

by Paul Seligman

Alfred A. Knopf / New York / 1972

Published in the United States by Alfred A. Knopf, Inc., New York,
and simultaneously in Canada by Random House of Canada
Limited, Toronto. Distributed by Random House, Inc., New York.
Manufactured in the United States of America

Library of Congress Cataloging in Publication Data
Seligman, Paul.
Debuts and farewells.
1. New York.
Metropolitan Opera.
I. Title.
ML1711.8.N3M597
782.1'09747'1
72-224
ISBN 0-394-47983-1

For the source of so many of the names, dates, and events,
and as a spur to recollection, I found invaluable
Irving Kolodin's *The Metropolitan Opera* (1953, 1966),
a finely written and monumental research work. Helpful, too,
were *The Golden Horseshoe: The Story of a Great Opera House*
(1965) by *Opera News* Editors and Frank Merkling, and
100 Great Operas and Their Stories (1957, 1960) by Henry W. Simon.
To Frank Merkling, Editor of *Opera News,*
goes my gratitude for his advice and encouragement.
Gerald Fitzgerald was most helpful with picture identifications.
My friend and a fine photographer, Bernard Gotfryd,
contributed much with his help in selecting the photographs.
Ira Teichberg's design set the visual style of the book.
Stuart Penney accomplished the difficult task
of printing over 250 negatives.
Coordinating all elements of the book
was my editor, Carol Janeway.
And to Elinor Alpern, dear Ellie, go my hearfelt
thanks for help with the manuscript and for providing
a calm sea when the going got rough.

This is a Borzoi Book
Published by Alfred A. Knopf, Inc.

Also by Paul Seligman Somehow It Works

CONTENTS

PREFACE

During the summer of 1953, a friend of mine, Marvin Farkas, invited me for the weekend to his father's house in Westhampton, Long Island. The adjoining cabana was occupied by Mr. and Mrs. Walter Surovy and their young son. Mrs. Surovy was better known as Risë Stevens, the reigning Carmen at the Metropolitan Opera, and their guest was Francis Robinson, then as now an assistant manager of the Met. That first meeting, which concluded with an invitation to see a performance, was to prove perhaps the most momentous of my life.

I was at that time editing the in-house publication of a large Fifth Avenue department store, and had that summer begun using a camera for the first time, mostly to illustrate articles in the magazine. One of its regular features was an interview with a celebrity/customer. It occurred to me now to do a story on Risë Stevens. I phoned the Metropolitan to ask Francis how to get in touch with her and was promptly invited in to hear _La Forza del Destino_. Up to that time I had seen only two operas, both at the Metropolitan. The first I remember vaguely—a _Traviata_ in 1948 or '49, seen from a seat in the balcony or family circle. I will never forget the second. It was on January 22, 1951, and I waited in line for hours to buy a standing-room ticket for that evening's performance, _Tristan und Isolde_, heralding the postwar return of Kirsten Flagstad.

After _La Forza_, I was invited in a number of times that autumn of 1953. One Saturday matinee was especially memorable. _Faust_ was being presented with Jussi Björling, whose glorious tenor voice I couldn't wait to hear. I also came prepared with a camera.

At the end of the first act, an announcement was made that Björling had become indisposed and that Thomas Hayward would take over as Faust. My camera came to mind. I quickly left my seat to seek out Francis's help to get backstage for pictures of Hayward preparing to go on—and so took my first photographs at the Metropolitan Opera. (One of these accompanies this preface and shows Robert Herman, then a stage assistant, and later an assistant manager, instructing Hayward.)

That matinee long ago may very well have been the genesis for this book. I was to come to the Met, cameras in hand, many times after that through the years, particularly for debuts and farewells. Always it was with the cooperation of Francis Robinson, for I could not have photographed at the House without his help: most of the time I was not on assignment; only in the sixties did I begin to receive commissions from Opera News to photograph complete operas during dress rehearsals. To Robinson goes my heartfelt appreciation.

After a few years, the prime motive for coming to photograph was a sense of personal mission—stuffy as that may sound. I also relished the challenge involved in capturing pictures that could never be repeated. After several years, it was evident I had begun to amass a comprehensive collection of photographs that documented one of the world's leading opera houses. I knew of no other photographer who was consistently going after those intimate glimpses that I felt truly presented the Met's ambience. Unlike newspaper and other magazine photographers, who came in for newsworthy events, or the official photographer whose duty it is to take formal portraits and performance pictures, I could attempt whatever I wished and was beholden to no one else's ideas about what I should record. My modus operandi: watch and wait, roam the corridors, climb the staircases, try to get backstage and into the dressing rooms. I took it as a great compliment when Ann Gordon, the Met's press associate, said to me, "...you were always going off on your own and not where we took you."

What I have strived for in my picture-taking is to capture, by existing light and with fast film and fast lenses, the drama and excitement at the House. I also wanted to document the company at work. The value of such a pictorial record can be the more appreciated if we look at photographs of the Old House at Broadway and 39th Street. Torn down six years ago, it exists no more—and I lament its passing. But the pictures can evoke memories for us all: the Old Met, creaking with age and restrictive in its function, did possess the character that comes with long life—and what a life!

The work of two photographers has been a source of inspiration to me through the years. I am always moved by the period-piece realism and revelation of history-tinged-by-nostalgia in the work of the pioneer photo-journalist Erich Salamon (who was to die in a German concentration camp in 1944). The Frenchman Henri Cartier-Bresson has gone beyond photo-journalism and into art by the beauty of his compositions and his perceptive delineations of character.

I do not know whether I was fortunate or not in taking up photography and my coverage at the Met at the same time. My developing of film could have been better in those early days; some of the photographs here of the Old House may be grainy and underexposed. I should point out, however, that shooting at the Metropolitan Opera—or in any theater—presents a photographer with some of the toughest lighting problems he will ever encounter. Stage productions are not lighted for photography. Expose for the bright areas and you lose subtle tones in the background; open up the lens to get the darker background and you produce chalky faces. And so one tries to decide which part of the stage is more important and thereby attempts to narrow the area. Compromise is the general rule. Luckily, Tri-X film and I arrived on the photographic scene at the same time. I began photographing at the Old House with Canon rangefinder cameras, to which in later years I added a Leica M2 and two Nikon F cameras with a range of lenses up to 300mm.

Looking back over the years of association with the Metropolitan, particular moments come vividly to mind. There were the hectic dashes by subway to get to the Old House in time, the bright, warm light of the Broadway entrance surrounded by the drab darkness of the garment center at night. Then the problem of where to stop and shoot first: if I spent too much time outside the House I would be missing the activity inside—the corridors, backstage, and the dressing rooms. It was usually a compromise of grabbing what I could out front, followed by a dash into the executive entrance on 39th Street.

Traveling with the company from Penn Station overnight to Atlanta in 1954 remains a vivid memory—several days in that lovely city and four operas in seventy-two hours. How pleasant to photograph at the Fox Theater, with no union restrictions, no threats from stagehands upon seeing a camera focused in their direction. Then there was a party at the Piedmont Driving Club on the last night of the company's stay. I ran out of film and began a frenzied rush by taxi to find an open drugstore where I could restock and return without having missed too much of the activity.

Twenty years of coming to two opera houses provoked in me all ranges of emotion, from the first feelings of eager anticipation to peaks of passionate involvement. Then, too, there were the downturns to frustration over pictures I couldn't get....But the peaks made up for the losses. A performance of Otello in 1958 with Mario Del Monaco, Renata Tebaldi, and Leonard Warren. I saw it from box one, which means that only about half the stage was visible to me. But what singing! And, in 1959, the towering figure of Herman Uhde during his superb performance in Wozzeck. Then there was the night in 1965 when I opened the side door to the auditorium at the Old House just a crack to observe the finale of Act II of Tosca—with Maria Callas and Tito Gobbi onstage.

This book exists because of the foresight and appreciation of a man, a gentle man, a fine writer and critic of music, particularly opera. I can't recall who it was who told me to take the book dummy to Herbert Weinstock at Knopf. He gathered it in and presented its case to the committee there. He would have been my editor and his would have been the text, not mine, for he was enthused with the idea of probing the subjects of the many photographs. This was not to be, however: Herbert Weinstock died suddenly, a few weeks after the contract was signed. This book is also for him.

PAUL SELIGMAN
MAY 1972

AN APPRECIATION

The bull ring is not the only arena with its moment of truth. Rudolf Bing has said that theater people are the one class in the world who must put up a fight every night for their existence. In the opera house, the theater on the grandest scale of all, and where everything is oversize—voices, emotions, hazards, triumphs—this fight becomes one of awesome proportions. Paul Seligman captures it in his stunning photographs; that is perhaps the most striking thing about this remarkable book.

He catches and conveys to us the supercharged atmosphere that reigns in different ways, both out front and backstage. With him we are almost painfully close to the prima donna in those few fearful and wonderful hours when a lifetime of work and renunciation is at stake. With him we escort her back to the dressing room and that curious aftermath which is a mixture of letdown and exhilaration, of exhaustion and renewal, of death and life. From a Seligman photograph you can tell as much about her as from a recording. Opera lovers long after us will be, as are we, most beholden to him.

FRANCIS ROBINSON
ASSISTANT MANAGER, METROPOLITAN OPERA

My first remembrance of opera goes back
to when I was growing up in Brooklyn and radio was
the prime means of entertainment. Every so often
"M'appari" from Flotow's *Martha* would come over the airwaves,
sending my father into a state of rapture and recollection of
having heard Caruso sing it at the Metropolitan Opera.
It was his favorite piece of music, as I recall,
and whenever I hear it I think of him.
It is to the memory of my father, and of my
mother, that I dedicate this book.

THE OLD HOUSE

The Old House

The old Metropolitan Opera House, built by and for men of wealth and social standing, was one of the great opera palaces. Filling the block made by Broadway and Seventh Avenue at 39th–40th Streets, it opened on October 22, 1883, a riotous baroque extravaganza of maroon and gold, decorated with lavish reliefs and painted cherubs—the whole crowned by a massive chandelier. Despite atrocious sight-lines and cramped backstage facilities, its acoustics were superb: there are those who remember how Enrico Caruso's voice would float echoing into the corridors.

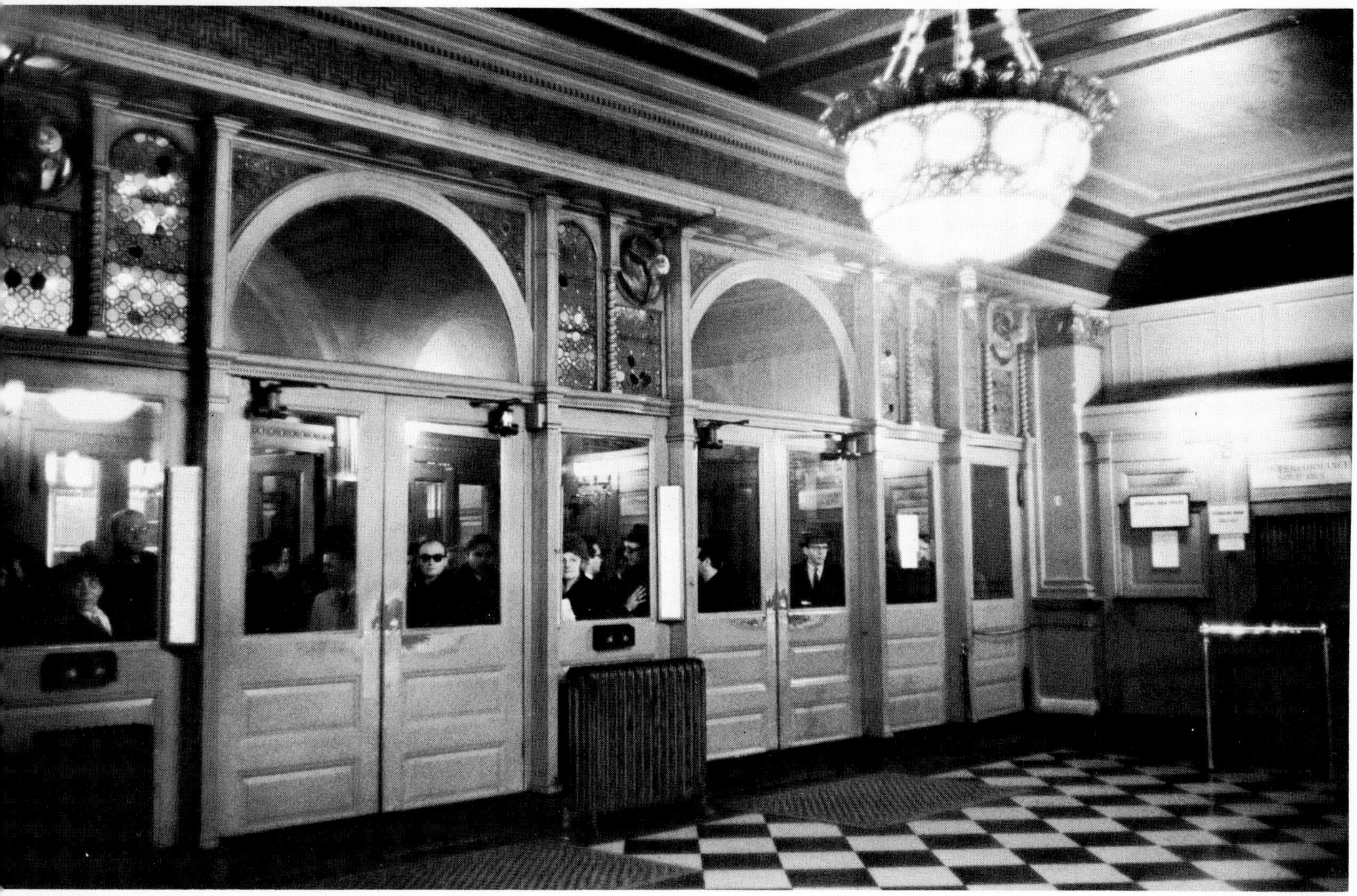

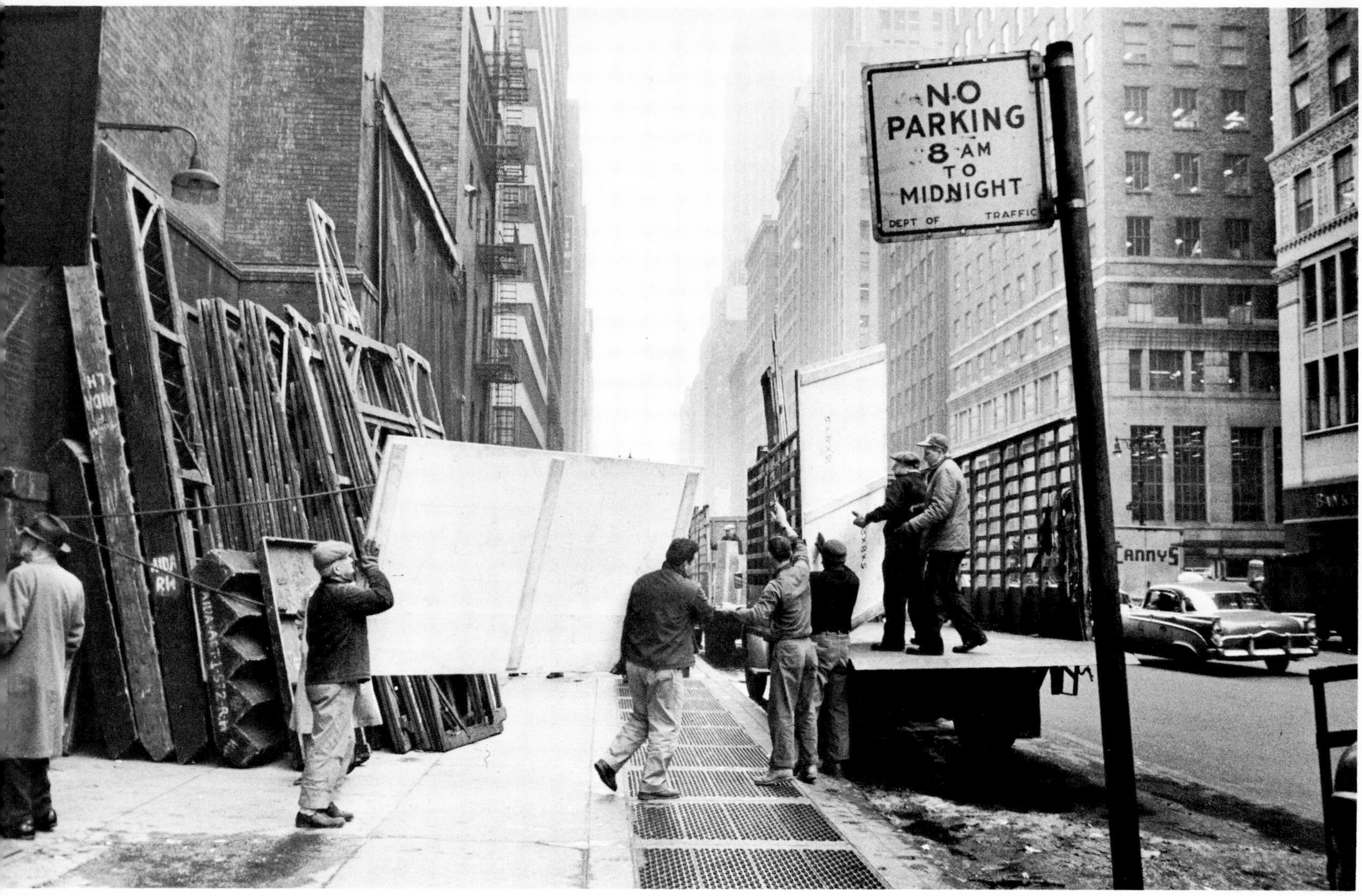
NO PARKING
8 AM
TO
MIDNIGHT
DEPT OF TRAFFIC

DURING PERFORMANCES
AND REHEARSALS
THIS DOOR IS TO BE USED ONLY
BY ARTISTS MANAGEMENT, HEADS
OF DEPARTMENTS & MUSICAL STAFF
CHORUS, BALLET, CREW &
SUPERS ARE REQUESTED
TO USE THE UPSTAGE DOOR
TO ENTER & LEAVE STAGE
EXIT

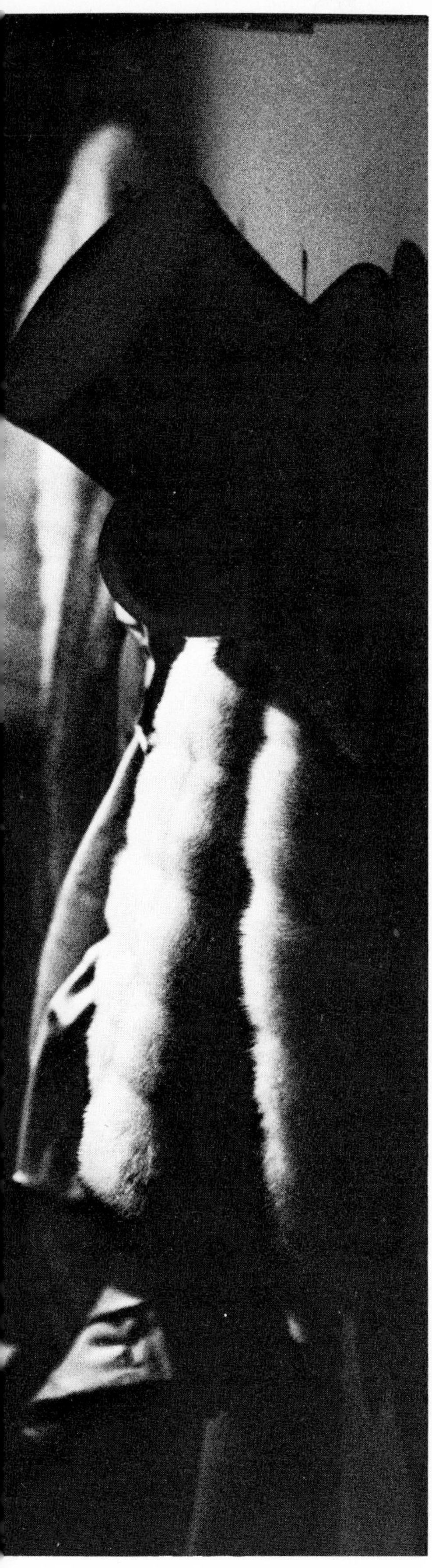

76

The "assembly room" of an earlier age found its reincarnation in the great restaurant Sherry's, with its celebrated flocked wallpaper and mirrored columns—a mecca for Broadway audiences.
Page 14: Metropolitan mezzo soprano Blanche Thebom (left), in tiara and full evening dress, mingles with such theatre people as Judith Anderson (upper right, with Met assistant manager Francis Robinson) and columnist Earl Wilson (lower right). Page 15: Mayor Robert Wagner (left) and New York's glamorous—who come to look, and be looked at.

Opening Nights

A radiant Renata Tebaldi, wrapped in ermine, sweeps past the 39th Street entrance on Opening Night, November 14, 1955, ten months after her debut—the epitome of all the glamour and excitement of a Metropolitan first night. Meanwhile, the sidewalks outside are jammed with arriving ticket-holders and those who have come merely to share the sparkle and perhaps to catch sight of a favorite star.

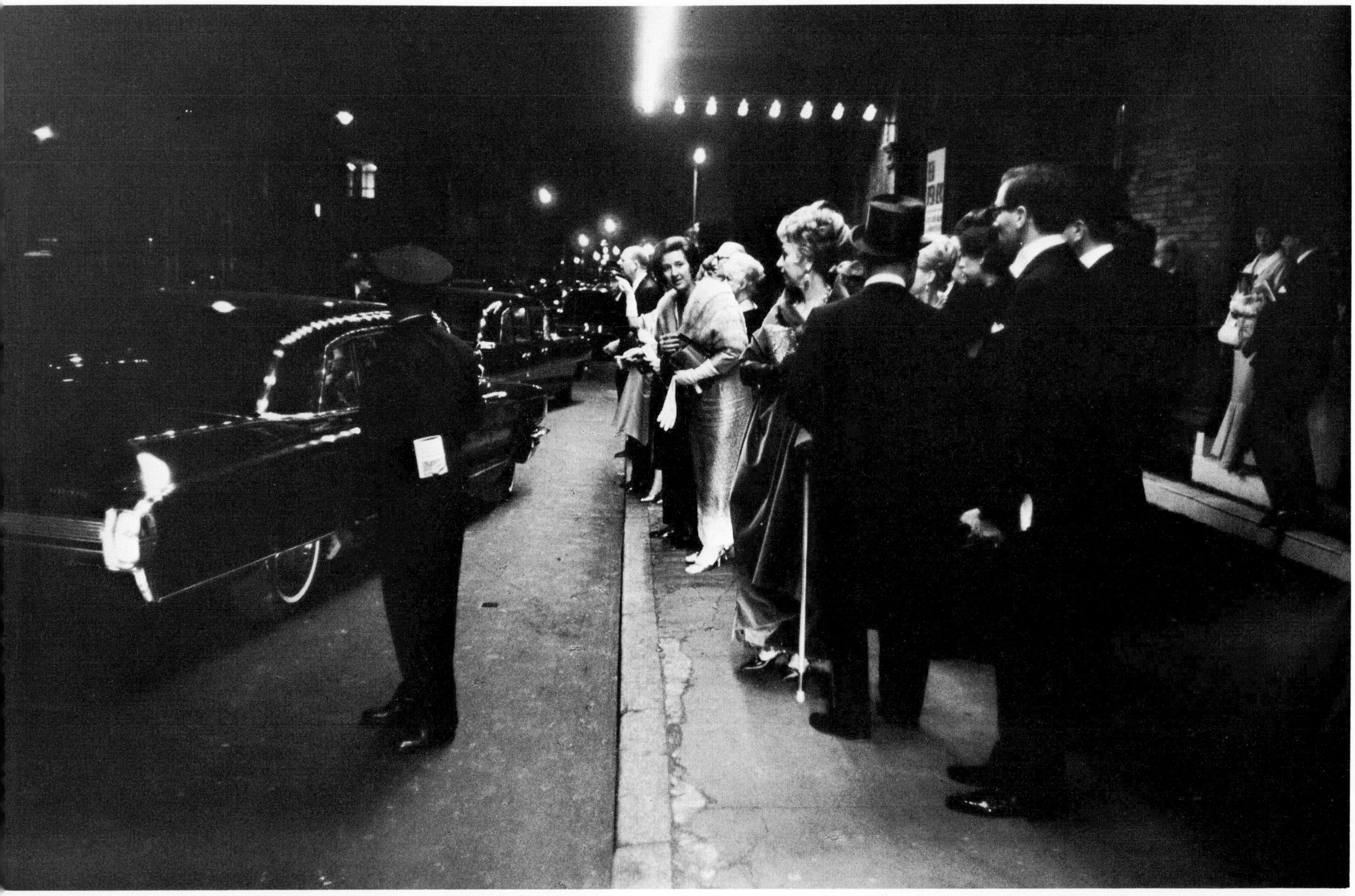

METROPOLITAN
OPERA
FRIDAY EVENING NOV 2nd
SUBSCRIPTION PERFORMANCE
SOIREE
LA BOHEME
METROPOLITAN
OPERA

October 26, 1959—the opening opera is Il Trovatore, *selected to start the season for the first time in the company's history. Leonard Warren, Giulietta Simionato, and Antonietta Stella take their bows at the end of a triumphant evening (page 20). Page 21, top: Simionato and Carlo Bergonzi. Bottom: the tragi-comic opening to the 1955 season—*The Tales of Hoffmann, *a frothy production that stars Alessio de Paolis, Sandra Warfield, Norman Scott, Mildred Miller, Martial Singher, Lucine Amara, and Richard Tucker.*

On Tour

The tour has always been part of the company's schedule. In the fifties, as many as nineteen cities saw the Met in a year, but by 1972 this number had shrunk to seven, due to rising costs. May 22, 1954—General Manager Rudolf Bing sees off one of the two opera trains after a stop in Washington, D.C. Later (page 24, top), he chats with choreographer Zachary Solov while Fernando Corena, Roberta Peters, and Cesare Valletti relax (lower right); also aboard (page 25) is Lily Pons. Ahead of them—Atlanta, with its Fox Theater on Peachtree Street, and four operas in three days.

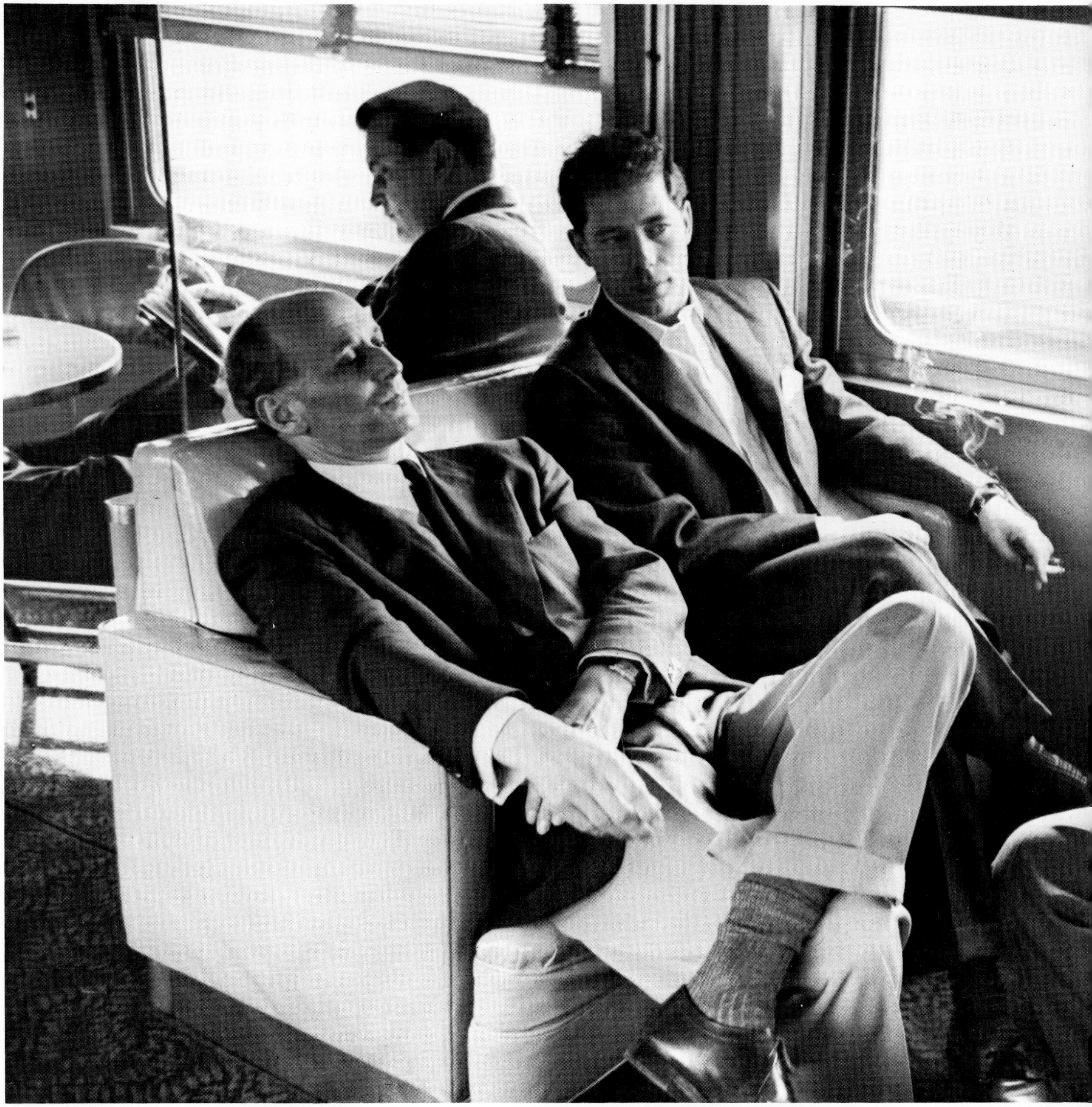

METROPOLITAN OPERA
ASSN.
SPRING TOUR
TRAIN 'B'
M010
M011
M013
M014
M015
M016

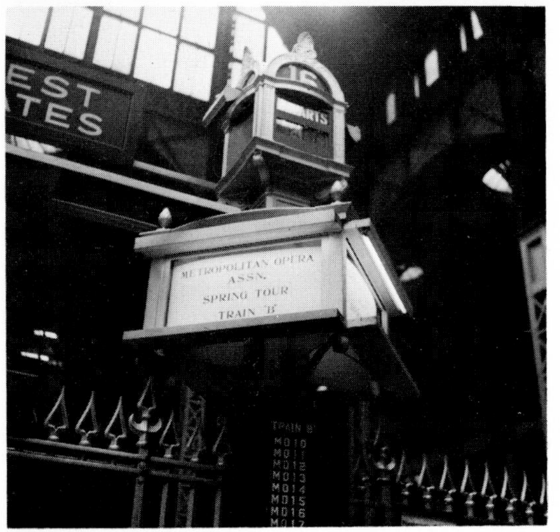

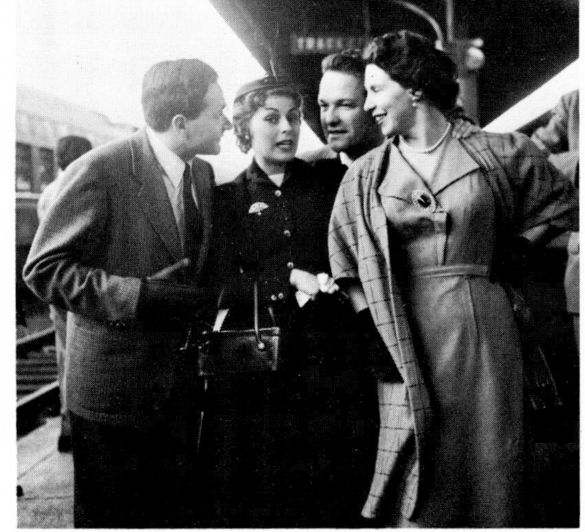

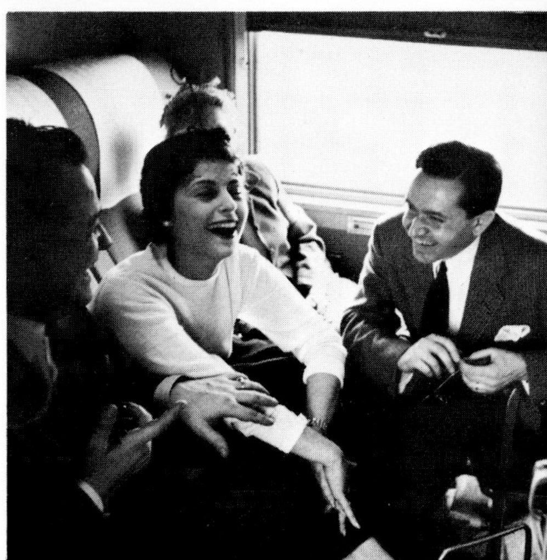

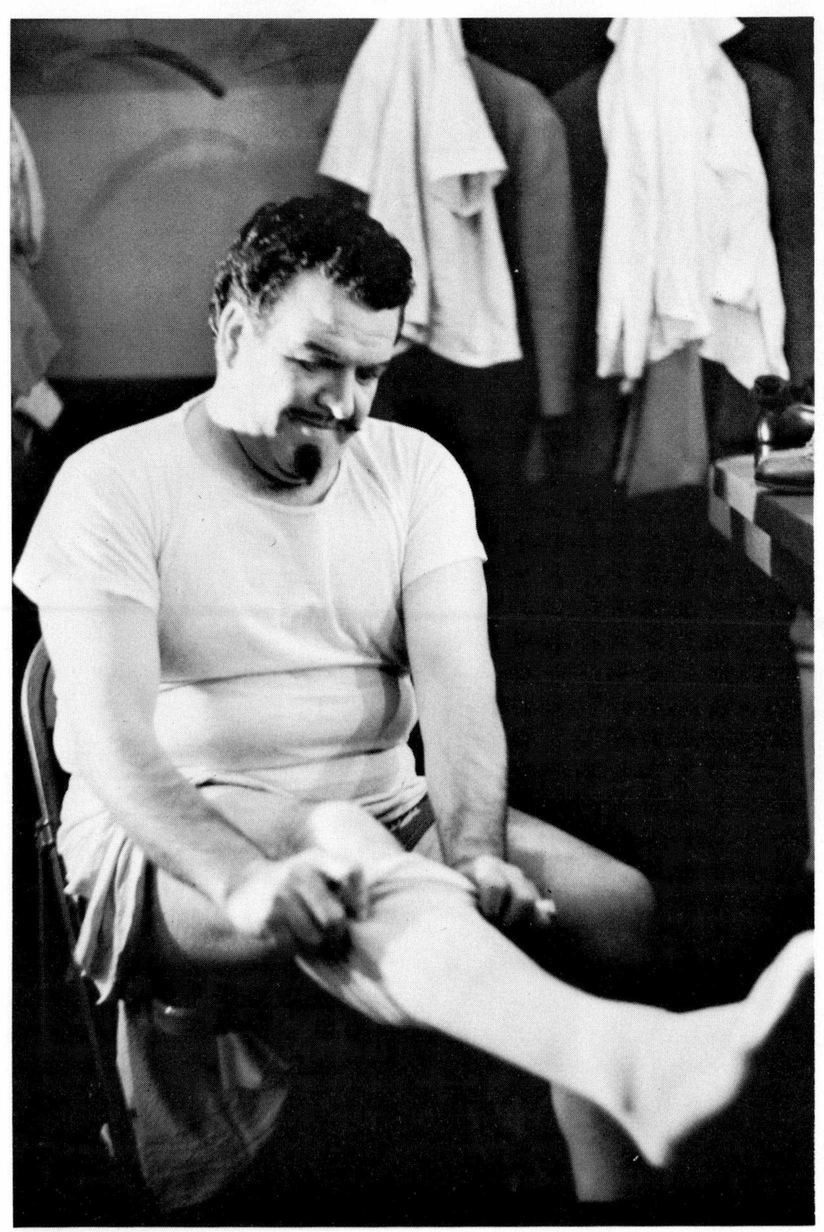

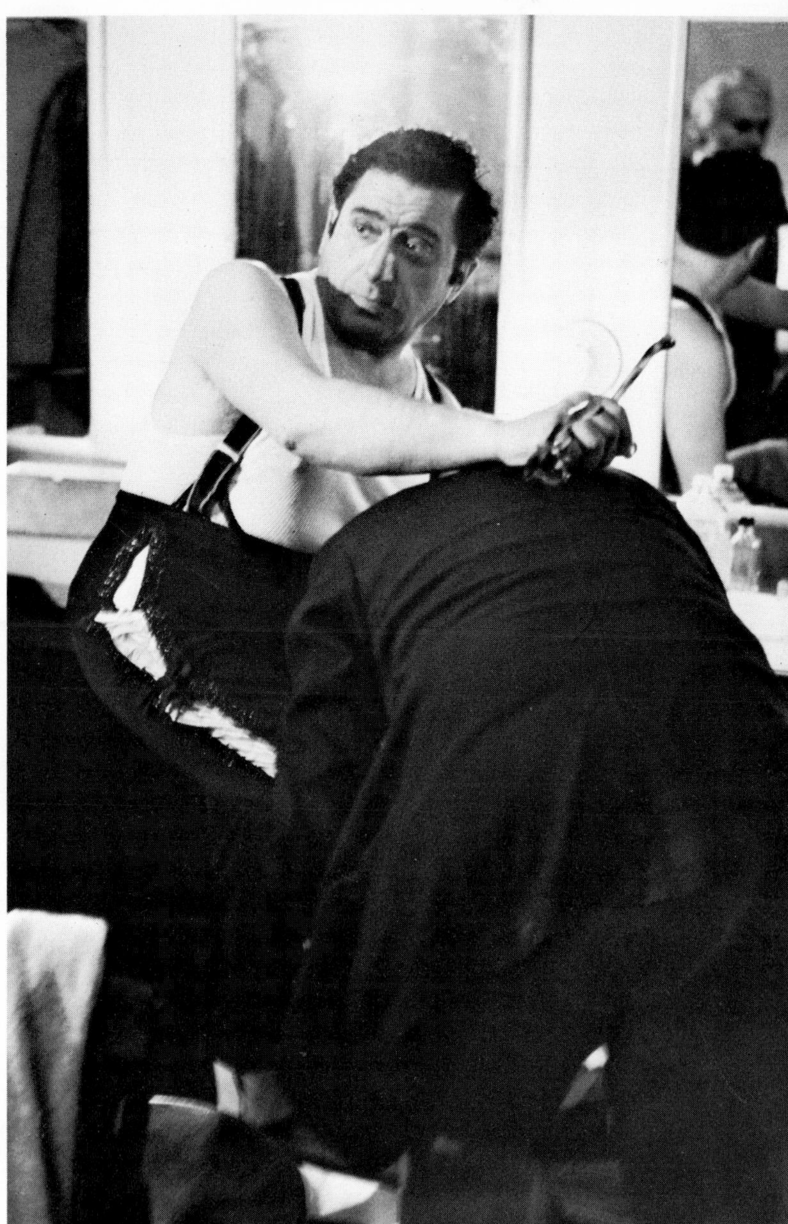

Backstage at the Fox Theater (page 26), Thomas Hayward and Jan Peerce dress for Lucia di Lammermoor. *Victoria de los Angeles has a word with Frank Guarrera (page 27, upper left); Cesare Siepi opts for cards (lower left). Jerome Hines and Eugene Conley (page 28 and page 29, upper left) prepare for* Faust, *Leonard Warren (upper right) for* La Forza del Destino. *Lower left: De los Angeles, with her husband, practices. Lower right: George London as Don Giovanni. Page 30: chorus for* La Forza; *props. Page 31: the ballet from* Faust; *the final party; (center, right) Warren, Fritz Stiedry, Zinka Milanov, and Richard Tucker.*

Debuts: Marian Anderson

January 7, 1955—a landmark occasion: a Negro is to sing a leading role with the company for the first time. Marian Anderson's Ulrica, in Verdi's Un Ballo in Maschera, *displays a voice perhaps past its peak, but one that sparkles with dramatic intensity. The cast (page 32, top) includes Richard Tucker, Zinka Milanov, Roberta Peters, and Leonard Warren. The audience claim Anderson as their own, and afterward there is a kiss from her mother (upper right). The great Helen Keller (bottom, page 32) is among the crowd.*

Debuts: Maria Callas

October 29, 1956—an electric evening: the debut of Maria Callas. She has already gained world fame with her performances at the Colón, Mexico City, La Scala, Covent Garden, and the Chicago Opera, 1945–55. Twice before, she has declined invitations to sing at the Met. Now she is here, in the role of Bellini's Norma, which she has made her own, with a cast that includes Fedora Barbieri and Mario Del Monaco. Later, poignant moments with husband Giovanni Meneghini (page 37) and Marlene Dietrich (pages 38–9).

Debuts: Joan Sutherland

November 26, 1961—the debut of Joan Sutherland in Lucia di Lammermoor. *Three years earlier, she had auditioned for the Met and been turned down. Since then, she has dazzled Covent Garden as Lucia in a performance that had British critics comparing her with Nellie Melba, and has given a New York concert that alerted American critics to her art. Franco Zeffirelli, who directed her London role, has influenced her interpretation, particularly of the "Mad Scene" (page 40, left). Richard Tucker is her Edgardo. Pages 44-5: in her dressing room, with husband and mentor Richard Bonynge.*

Martinelli's 50th Anniversary

November 20, 1963—the fiftieth anniversary, to the day, of Giovanni Martinelli's debut with the company as Rodolfo in La Bohème. *A Guild Benefit is arranged to do honor to his glorious New York career. Onstage, as he speaks his thanks (page 46), are many colleagues with whom he has sung over the years, including Bidú Sayão, Rose Bampton, and John Brownlee. Afterward, he stands next to the bust of himself in the House. This great tenor, for whom the company revived* Otello *in 1937 after a twenty-five-year absence from the repertory, died in 1969.*

Callas Returns

Disputes and recriminations led to the dismissal of Maria Callas by Rudolf Bing in 1958, but seven years later the wounds were healed. March 19 and 25, 1965—she returns in performances of Tosca *that break box-office records. Those lucky enough to obtain tickets —including Jacqueline Kennedy (page 48, upper left)—are privileged to see one of the most unforgettable productions ever staged at the Old House. Tito Gobbi is Scarpia (page 48, lower left). Franco Corelli sings Cavaradossi the first night; Richard Tucker, the second. Onstage afterward (pages 50-1), her hands embrace Bing in reconciliation.*

Milanov's Farewell

April 16, 1966—Zinka Milanov gives her farewell performance, as Maddalena in Andrea Chénier, *after a career of superlatives with the Met. Her 28 years in the company, 424 performances (125 on tour), and four Opening Nights are a record exceeded by only four prima donnas: Emma Eames, Emmy Destin, Rosa Ponselle, and Elisabeth Rethberg. Co-stars Anselmo Colzani and Richard Tucker add to the acclaim (upper right), and the entire company, audience, and Board of Directors join in homage to her.*

Rehearsals

Many rehearsals at the Old House were done on the roof extensions, built in 1909 and 1921. Pages 54-7: a day of preparation for the première of La Perichole, *which opened on December 21, 1956, a novelty work for New York operagoers. Cyril Ritchard directed, Rolf Gérard did the sets, and Jean Morel conducted the company in Maurice Valency's fine English translation. In these photographs, one—page 54, bottom—is of particular interest: along with Cyril Ritchard, Patrice Munsel, and Theodor Uppman is a tenor (seated) who would go on to greater things—James McCracken.*

Don Giovanni

October 31, 1957, the Met's first new production of Don Giovanni *in nearly thirty years, and one of Rudolf Bing's finest achievements. Sets are by Eugene Berman and direction by Herbert Graf; Karl Böhm makes his debut conducting a fine cast led by Cesare Siepi in the title role. Eleanor Steber is Dona Anna; Roberta Peters, Zerlina; Lisa Della Casa, Elvira; Theodor Uppman, Masetto; Cesare Valletti, Ottavio; Fernando Corena, Leporello; and Giorgio Tozzi, the Commendatore. Pages 58-65: 1963 photographs of most of the earlier cast. Gabriella Tucci is a later Elvira (above, center) and William Wildermann a later Commendatore (page 62, left).*

Pages 62–3: in the final sequences of the opera, Siepi's Don Giovanni is confronted and condemned by the Commendatore's statue before being swept down to Hell. Pages 64–5: in a lighter mood backstage, Steber and Della Casa relax and clown a little.

The Marriage of Figaro

If Don Giovanni *is ranked by some as the greatest of Mozart's operas,* The Marriage of Figaro *is the best loved in the canon. Since 1959, the Met has used Cyril Ritchard's staging with great success. In this 1964 performance, Cesare Siepi is Figaro; Hermann Prey, Count Almaviva; Lisa Della Casa, the Countess; Teresa Stratas, Cherubino; Gladys Kriese, Marcellina; and Elfego Esparza, Dr. Bartolo. Above, center: Judith Raskin, as Susanna, dominates a scene with Figaro.*

Die Fledermaus and Others

Operetta at the Met? Shocking to some purists, nineteen performances of Die Fledermaus *—a record for one work in any single season—were given in 1950–1, all of them sold out. Garson Kanin directed, Howard Dietz provided a new English translation, Rolf Gérard did the sets, and Eugene Ormandy conducted. The cast included Richard Tucker, Patrice Munsel, Ljuba Welitch, Risë Stevens, John Brownlee, and Jack Gilford as Frosch. In 1962–3, the production is still going strong—Jean Madeira (above, seated, in uniform), as Prince Orlofsky, entertains his guests.*

Pages 70-1: Leontyne Price in Ernani; *Leonie Rysanek and Richard Tucker in* Un Ballo in Maschera; *Eileen Farrell and Franco Corelli in* Andrea Chénier; *Fernando Corena and Cesare Siepi in* The Barber of Seville. *Pages 72-3: (top) Price and Cornell MacNeil in* Ernani; *(bottom) the Jacobin mob in* Chénier; *(top) Kurt Baum (high center) as Radames in* Aida; *(bottom) Rosalind Elias and Licia Albanese in* Madama Butterfly. *Pages 74-5: Anna Moffo in* Lucia di Lammermoor. *Pages 76-7: Renata Tebaldi in* Adriana Lecouvreur; *the ballet from* Un Ballo in Maschera.

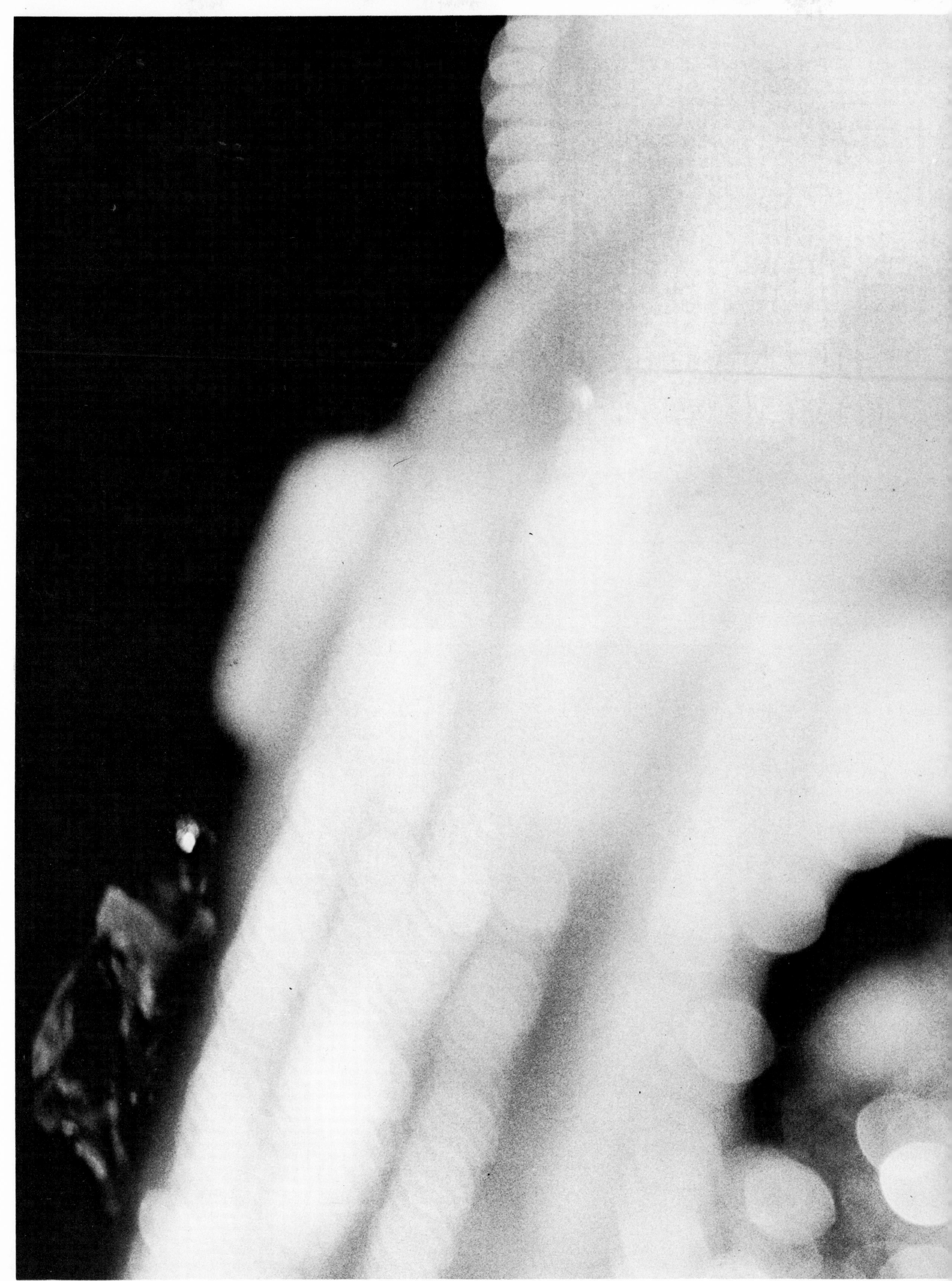

Conductors Par Excellence

Ernest Ansermet and Pierre Monteux, revered maestros who brought cachet to the company's French repertoire. Ansermet, born the year the Old House opened, conducted Pelléas et Mélisande *as his first opera there on November 30, 1962; he poses after leading the company during opening ceremonies at Philharmonic Hall. Monteux returned to the house in 1953, after thirty-four years' absence, to conduct the* Faust *that replaced the one he led at his Metropolitan debut in 1917; here, on Opening Night, November 14, 1955, he is about to begin the first new* Tales of Hoffmann *at the Met in thirty years.*

The Old House Closes

Saturday, April 22, 1966—the last day there will ever be opera at the Old House. The former "palace" is now a grime-covered shell, prey to the wreckers. The company has outgrown its old home, whose swan song will be a matinee performance of La Bohème. *For days the lines stretch out as devotees queue for tickets to the matinee opera and the evening's Gala Farewell. The first performance at Lincoln Center—a student matinee of Puccini's* La Fanciulla del West*—has already taken place eleven days earlier. Eighty-three years of operatic history are drawing to their close.*

The Gala Farewell

The best seats went for almost twenty times the normal price—$200—and company revenue was a record $290,000. Fifty-seven singers and eleven conductors take part, the proceedings led off by Leopold Stokowski with a pulsating "Entrance of the Guests" from Tannhaüser. *Then come the guests of honor, almost forty past artists of the Met. From Marian Anderson and Lotte Lehmann at the evening's start to the entire company singing "Auld Lang Syne" as the golden curtain closes at 1:15 a.m. next morning, it is a farewell in the grand manner, full of laughter, tears, and heart-tugging emotion.*

Four of the soloists at the farewell: Birgit Nilsson, who sings "Brünnhilde's Immolation" (Götterdämmerung); *Leontyne Price, "D'amor sull' ali rosee"* (Il Trovatore); *Roberta Peters, "Una voce poco fa"* (The Barber of Seville); *and Sándor Kónya, "Preislied"* (Die Meistersinger).

Vocal ensembles at the farewell: (page 86, left to right) Giorgio Tozzi, Delia Regal, and Jan Peerce; Régine Crespin and Biserka Cvejic; Renata Tebaldi and Franco Corelli; Mary Ellen Pracht, Joann Grillo, Gladys Kriese, Theodor Uppman, and George Shirley; (page 87, left to right) John Alexander, Mignon Dunn, Eleanor Steber, Blanche Thebom, and Clifford Harvuot; Teresa Stratas, Mildred Miller, and Frank Guarrera; Jerome Hines, Gabriella Tucci, and Nicolai Gedda; Judith Raskin, Rosalind Elias, and Montserrat Caballé.

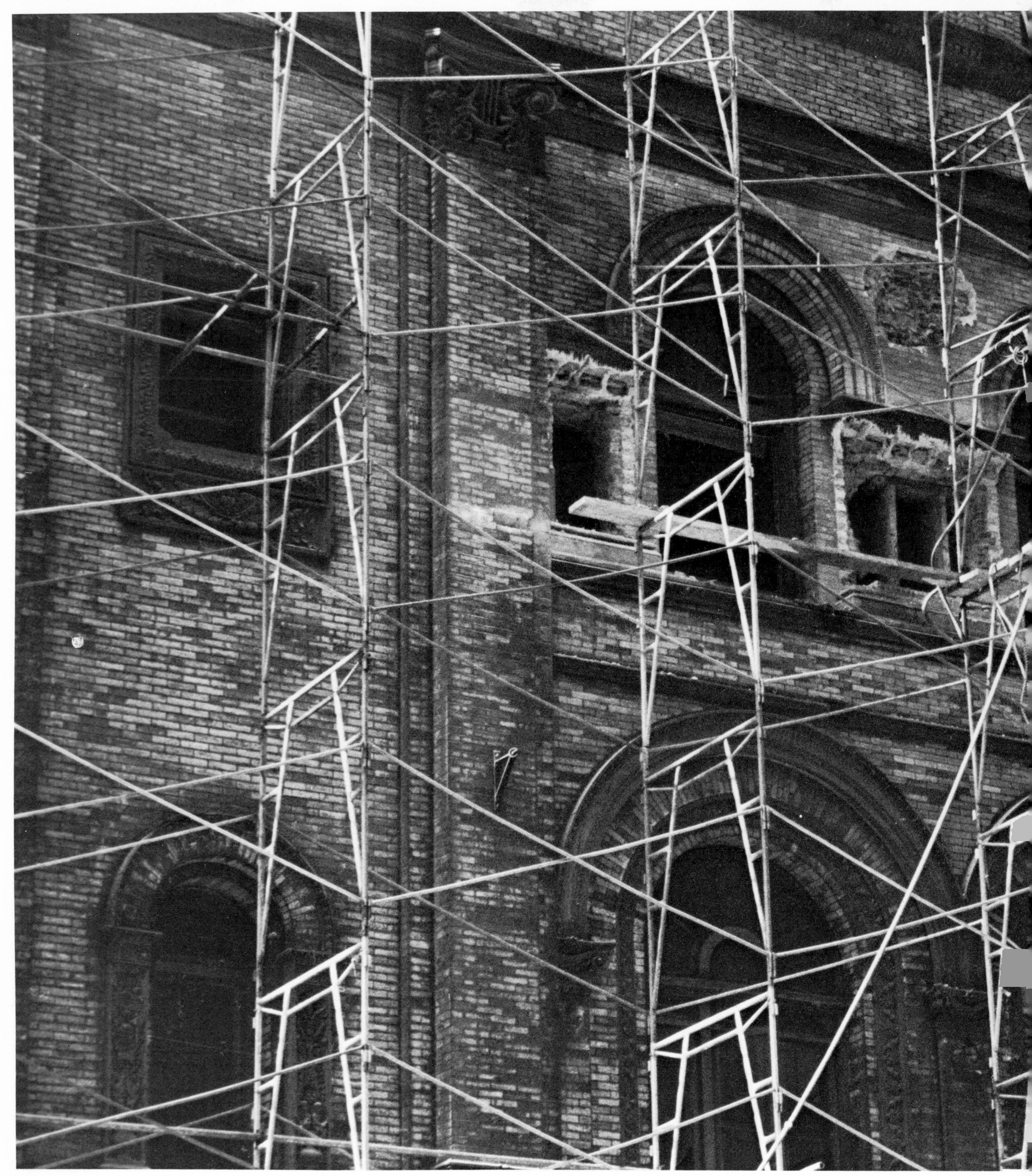

The Old House Comes Down

January 1967—with the company settled in its new, 64th Street home—the wreckers go to work. The facade becomes a mass of scaffolding, despite all the efforts of such people as soprano Licia Albanese (page 94, top) and the Old Met Corporation to buy and preserve the building as a home for ballet and other cultural activities. Carnegie Hall had been saved some years before—it was still functional. But the Met is viewed as an impractical antique. Chunks of gilded plaster cherubs are sold, as is an old portrait of Lucrezia Bori (page 95, bottom). Nostalgic fans salvage what they can.

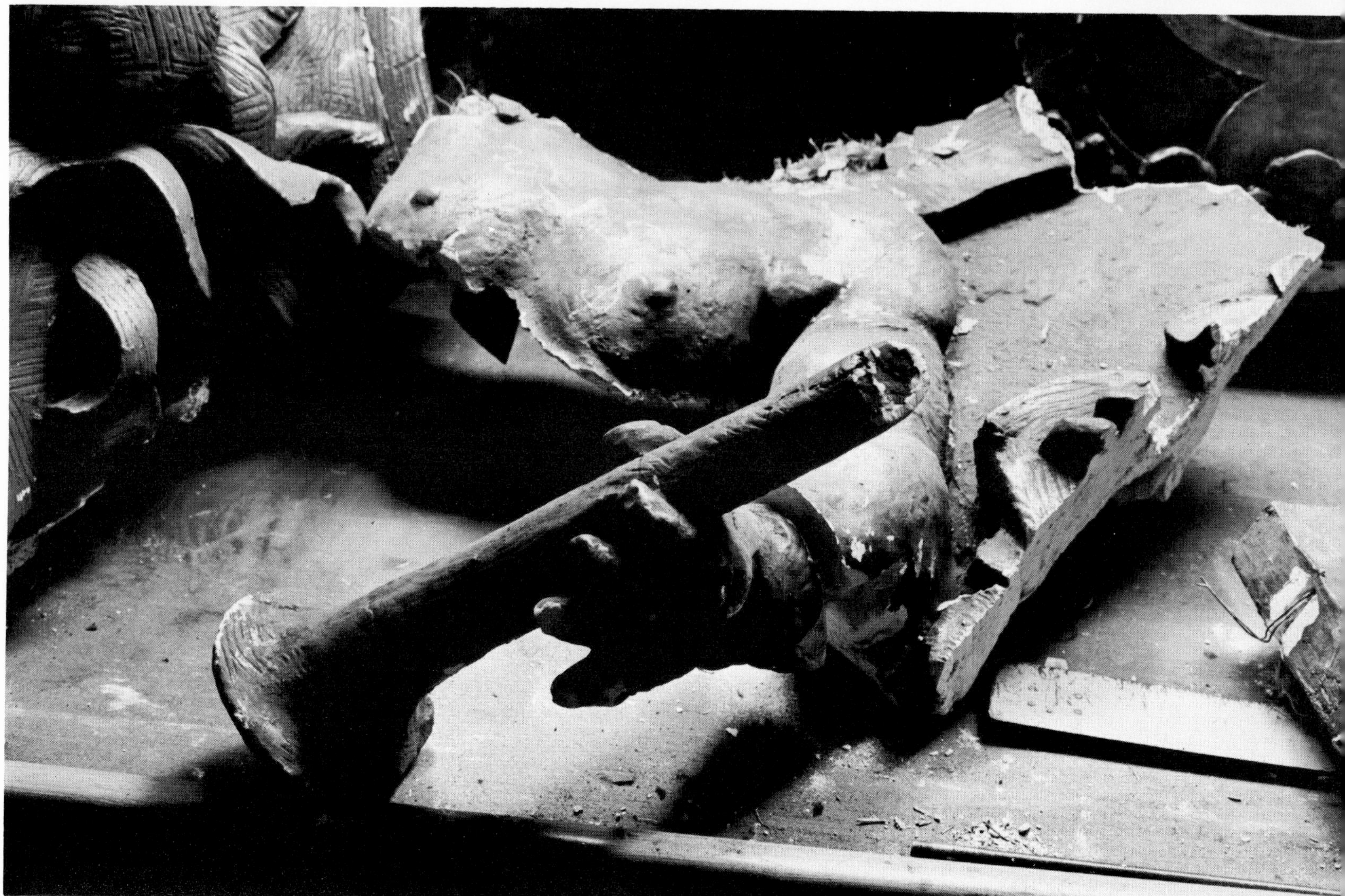

THE NEW HOUSE

The New House Rises

The deficiencies of the Old House had long given rise to dreams of a replacement. 1951 saw the first glimpse of a chance to move uptown to a site at Columbus Circle, but this fell through. Then, in 1958, came the Lincoln Square Urban Renewal Project for the Performing Arts. Ground for the New House was broken on May 14, 1959, in the presence of President Eisenhower. Above: the building complex in 1963; the Metropolitan Opera House, rising to form the central bulk, was completed in September 1966.

Inaugural at Lincoln Center

September 16, 1966—a new opera, Antony and Cleopatra, *commissioned from Samuel Barber to celebrate the event, and a dazzling crowd to complete the occasion. John D. Rockefeller III, Chairman of the Board of Lincoln Center, is here (page 101, upper right) with Rudolf Bing to show Mrs. Lyndon Johnson the building. Marc Chagall, whose two immense paintings adorn the grand tier, is among those present (lower right). The audience crowd the great staircase (page 100, left) and admire the chandeliers—a gift from the Austrian government.*

METROPOLITAN OPERA
DER FREISCHUTZ
METROPOLITAN OPERA
GAETANO DONIZETTI
L'ELISIR D'AMORE
METROPOLITAN OPERA
CHARLES GOUNOD
FAUST
METROPOLITAN OPERA
MONDAY EVENING, OCTOBER 25 at 8:00
SUBSCRIPTION PERFORMANCE
FIRST TIME THIS SEASON
WOLFGANG AMADEUS MOZART
COSI FAN TUTTE
CONDUCTOR, JOHN PRITCHARD
STAGED BY HENRY BUTLER
SETS and COSTUMES DESIGNED BY ROLF GERARD
FIORDILIGI . . . . . TERESA ZYLIS GARA
DORABELLA . . . . . ROSALIND ELIAS
DESPINA . . . . . TERESA STRATAS
FERRANDO . . . . . PIETRO BOTTAZZO
GUGLIELMO . . . . . TOM KRAUSE
DON ALFONSO . . . . . FERNANDO CORENA
METROPOLITAN OPERA
THURSDAY EVENING, OCTOBER 21 at 8:00
SUBSCRIPTION PERFORMANCE
GAETANO DONIZETTI
L'ELISIR D'AMORE
CONDUCTOR, CARLO FRANCI
STAGED BY NATHANIEL MERRILL
SETS and COSTUMES DESIGNED BY ROBERT O'HEARN
RERI GRIST
LUIGI ALVA
MARIO SERENI
FERNANDO CORENA
CAROL WILCOX
CHOREOGRAPHY BY TODD BOLENDER

25th Anniversaries: Richard Tucker

Tucker, born in Brooklyn, began his career as a cantor; he made his Metropolitan debut on January 25, 1945, in La Gioconda*, evoking comparisons with Beniamino Gigli. On April 11, 1970, the company pays homage to him. Tucker sings one act from each of three operas for which he is noted:* La Traviata*, with Joan Sutherland;* La Gioconda *(page 111, second from top, right), with Renata Tebaldi; and* Aida *(third from top), with Leontyne Price (far right). Molinari-Pradelli conducts, and Lowell Wadmond, Chairman of the Board, with Rudolf Bing, congratulates the star.*

25th Anniversaries: Robert Merrill

Robert Merrill—like Richard Tucker a native of Brooklyn—first considered a career in baseball, but he entered and won the "Auditions of the Air"—which led to his Metropolitan debut on December 14, 1945, singing the elder Germont in La Traviata. *Twenty-five years later, October 21, 1970, he repeats that performance, with Joan Sutherland as Violetta and Carlo Bergonzi as Alfredo (bottom, center). Eight of his many Violettas are onstage to congratulate him, Rudolf Bing comes up to stand with Joan Sutherland, there are kisses all around, and afterward—of course—a party.*

25th Anniversaries: Regina Resnik

One of the first young singers to move to the Met from the New York City Opera at City Center, Bronx-born Regina Resnik made her debut in Il Trovatore *on December 6, 1944, replacing an indisposed Zinka Milanov as Leonora. A most intelligent and versatile singer, she went on to produce and direct opera in Europe. For her 25th-anniversary performance, she sings her world-renowned Carmen, with Sándor Kónya (right) as Don José and Robert Merrill as Escamillo. Between acts (pages 116-17), she receives a silver bowl and congratulations from Rudolf Bing and the company.*

25th Anniversaries: Dorothy Kirsten

Of the four singers whose 25th anniversaries were observed on the Metropolitan stage during 1970-1, three were born in New York City and one seventeen miles away—in Montclair, New Jersey. Dorothy Kirsten's career began with touring companies and a stint in Italy as protégée of Grace Moore, then she came to the Met by way of the City Center. Having made her debut as Mimi in La Bohème, *December 1, 1945, she delights audiences with it twenty-five years later; Sándor Kónya (left) is her Rodolfo. At far right is Mario Sereni.*

The 1971-72 Season: Tristan und Isolde

Rudolf Bing's final season at the Met may rank as his greatest. Of his eighty-five new productions, seven were seen, including Wagner's Tristan und Isolde*—which opened on November 18 to spectacular reviews. Birgit Nilsson and Jess Thomas are the lovers, in the shipboard confrontation (left); Irene Dalis, as Brangaene, stands at Nilsson's right. Backstage, the stars relax (pages 126-7). Thomas Stewart (page 125) is Kurwenal. Above, top and center: the "Liebesnacht" duet. Lower right: the "Liebestod." Erich Leinsdorf conducts, seen here in rehearsal (page 124, bottom).*

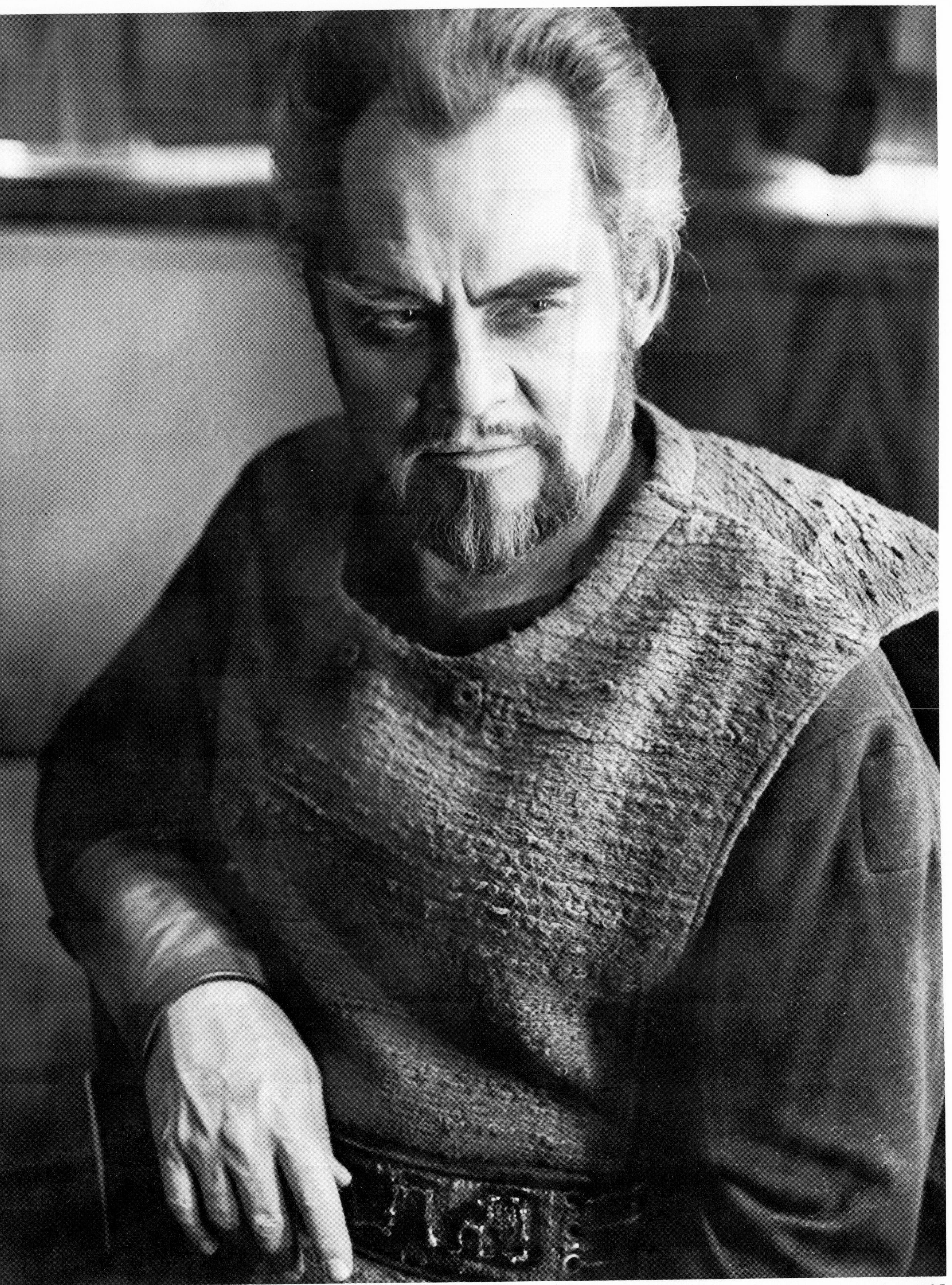

Die Meistersinger

October 18, 1962, witnessed the opening of the finest Meistersinger *in a generation, designed and directed by Robert O'Hearn and Nathaniel Merrill. The production is seen again in the 1971-2 season, with Giorgio Tozzi and Pilar Lorengar as Hans Sachs and Eva (page 130), Benno Kusche as Beckmesser (page 131, top), and James King as Walther (page 131, bottom, extreme left, in the final ensemble). An Act II set with Sachs's cottage at center stage allows the action between Eva and Walther, Beckmesser's serenade, the entry of the Nightwatchmen, and the street riot (above) to flow on unimpeded.*

Così Fan Tutte

November 3, 1971—the first performance of Mozart's Cosi Fan Tutte *to be sung in Italian at the Metropolitan Opera since the twenties. Teresa Zylis-Gara, Teresa Stratas, and Rosalind Elias are Fiordiligi, Despina, and Dorabella (page 132, top left); (bottom left) Pietro Bottazzo, Tom Krause, and Fernando Corena (far left) as Ferrando, Guglielmo, and Don Alfonso. Sets are by Rolf Gérard, from the original 1951-2 production by Alfred Lunt.*

Samson and Delilah, Rigoletto, Falstaff

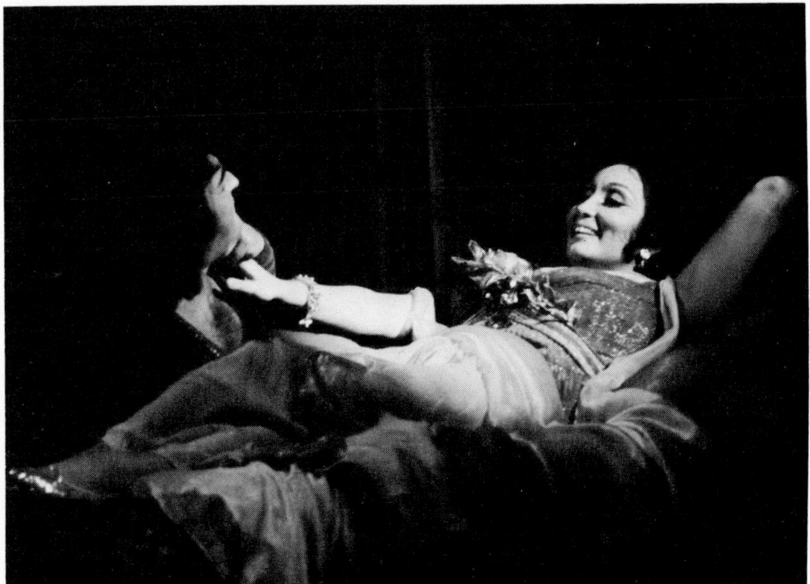

Samson and Delilah *finally entered the regular repertory of the Met in 1915, having previously been sung as an oratorio in deference to the popular prejudice against portraying biblical characters onstage—a far cry it must have been from the 1971 "Bacchanale" (left) or the seduction scene with Mignon Dunn and Richard Tucker (right). Page 136: Renata Scotto, singing Gilda, confesses her affair with the Duke to her heartbroken father, Rigoletto (Cornell MacNeil). Pages 138-9: Geraint Evans as Falstaff has a conquest in mind as he woos Alice Ford, sung by Renata Tebaldi.*

Salome, Tosca, La Fille du Régiment, and Others

Salome, *one of the most provocative of operas, provides Leonie Rysanek with a virtuoso role, blazing out of the darkness in the "Dance of the Seven Veils." Pages 142-3: Tito Gobbi and Grace Bumbry in the Scarpia-Tosca confrontation. In a quite different mood,* La Fille du Régiment *(pages 144-5), back after thirty years, with Joan Sutherland and Luciano Pavarotti, Regina Resnik (upper right), and Ljuba Welitch (lower right). Page 146: Weber's* Der Freischütz, *Act III (top); and* Hansel and Gretel *(bottom), with Teresa Stratas and Rosalind Elias. Page 147: Judith Blegen in the death scene from Debussy's* Pelléas et Mélisande.

Opera in the Park

*When Lewisohn Stadium closed in 1967, the Met moved its summer concert performances to the city's large parks. That first season was an all-Puccini affair—*La Boheme, Madama Butterfly, *and* Tosca, *and the series became a huge success as an annual event. At the Sheep Meadow in Central Park, June 30, 1970, Parks Commissioner August Heckscher (upper right) greets the crowd. Anna Moffo is Lucia and Frank Guarrera is Ashton in Donizetti's* Lucia di Lammermoor.

Informal Portraits

Offstage . . . Jerome Hines awaits his call as Colline in La Bohème. *Page 152: (top) music critics Alan Rich, George Morshon, and Harold Schonberg; (bottom) Anna Moffo, Renata Tebaldi, Licia Albanese, Gabriella Tucci, and Renata Scotto at the Merrill 25th. Page 153: (top) Franco Corelli and Birgit Nilsson after* Tosca, *June 1970; (bottom) Mignon Dunn is made up as Delilah. Page 154: (top) Carlo Bergonzi and Martina Arroyo, after* Ernani, *Opening Night 1970; (bottom) Pilar Lorengar as Agathe, after* Der Freischütz. *Page 155: (top) Luciano Pavarotti as Tonio, after* La Fille du Régiment; *(bottom) Ruggiero Raimondi at his Metropolitan debut in* Ernani.

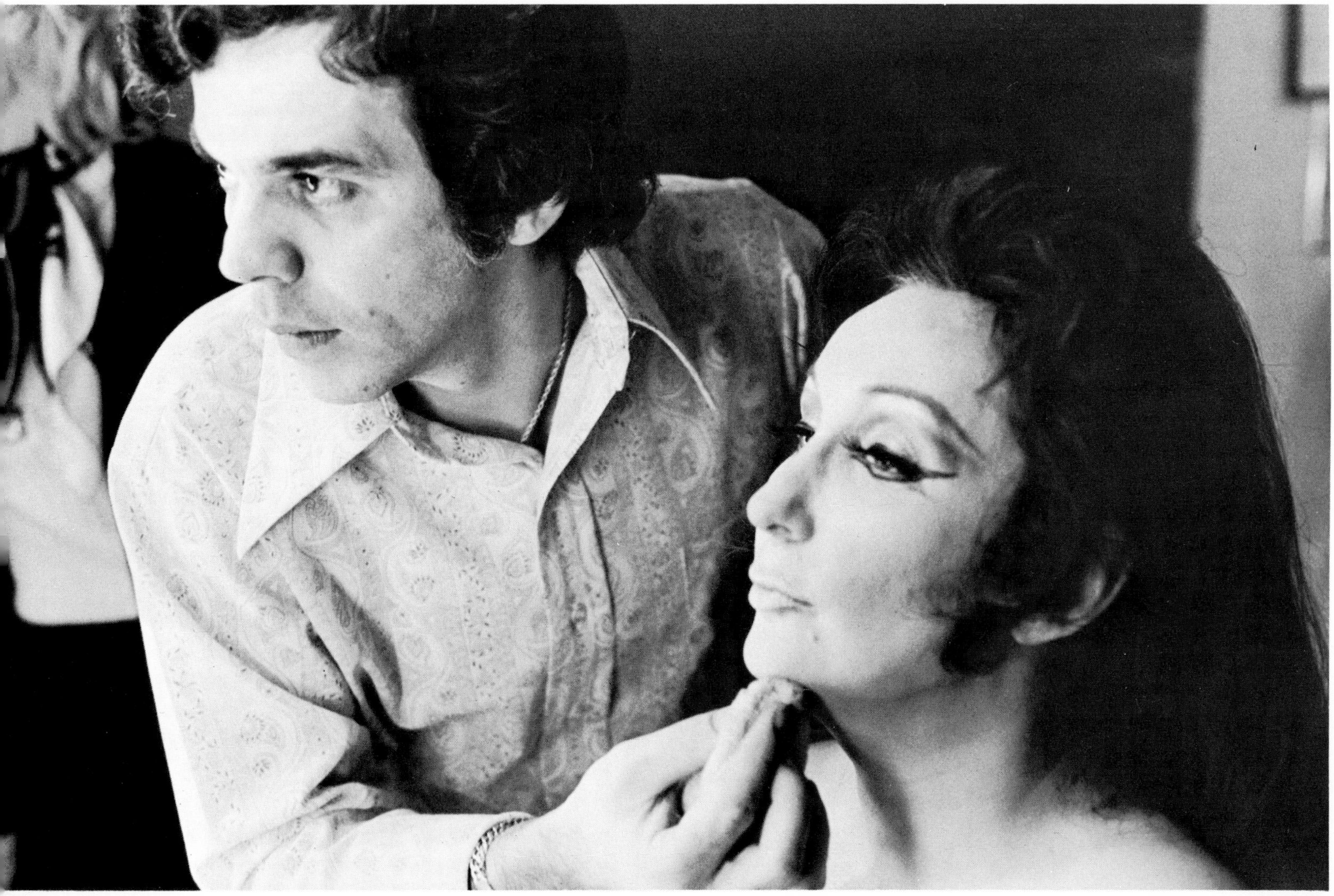

Page 156: Rosalind Elias, dressed as Dorabella, for Così Fan Tutte; *Marilyn Horne, as Adalgisa, ready to go on in* Norma. *Page 157: Grace Bumbry, resplendent as Princess Eboli, for* Don Carlo; *Renata Scotto, a gentle Gilda, between acts of* Rigoletto.

Page 158: Placido Domingo in his dressing room on Opening Night, 1971, Don Carlo; *Jon Vickers as Don José in Bizet's* Carmen. *Page 159: a smiling Mario Sereni, Marcello in* La Boheme; *Sherrill Milnes ready for the role of Don Carlos in* Ernani.

Sir Rudolf Bing

November 9, 1971, brought Rudolf Bing a knighthood from the British Crown—a fitting honor for a man whose successful career in operatic administration goes back to the twenties. In 1950 he began a twenty-two-year tenure at the Metropolitan Opera. Always controversial, he has lengthened the season from eighteen to thirty-one weeks and brought leading directors and designers into the work of the company. In his office, he confers with assistants Paul Jeretski and Robert Herman (page 162, bottom) and entertains Prime Minister Golda Meir and Mayor John Lindsay (page 163, bottom).

Don Carlo, Bing's Last Opening Night

*September 20, 1971—*Don Carlo. *Rudolf Bing's choice for his first Opening Night, in 1950, and one of his finest productions, starts his last year as General Manager. Cesare Siepi repeats his 1950 debut role of Philip II (page 165, upper left; and lower right with John Macurdy); Robert Merrill repeats his 1950 Rodrigo, and Lucine Amara her 1950 debut as the Celestial Voice. Pages 166-7: later, at an intermission with his successor, the late Göran Gentele (left), Kurt Waldheim, Secretary-General of the United Nations (center, leaning forward), and Rafael Kubelik (end of table, on his right).*

Otello, Bing's Last New Production

March 25, 1972—a new production of Verdi's brooding masterwork: a brilliant Franco Zeffirelli-Peter Hall design and costuming with which to end twenty-two years' work with the Metropolitan Opera. Zeffirelli also directed, with a superb cast led by James McCracken as Otello, in one of the most famous interpretations of our day. Sherrill Milnes sings his first Iago (page 168, top left), and Teresa Zylis-Gara is Desdemona.

Gala Farewell to Rudolf Bing

April 22, 1972—a musical salute to the General Manager. Six conductors perform, among them Karl Böhm (page 170, upper left) and James Levine (top, center). Page 171, upper right: Rudolf Bing whistles an alert to some prominent guests as an intermission draws to a close. The singers include (pages 170-1) Pavarotti, Sutherland, McCracken, (page 172, top) Domingo, Caballé, Price, (bottom) Corelli, Zylis-Gara, Merrill, Tucker (page 173, top) Enrico De Giuseppe, Amara, Siepi, (bottom) Crespin.

Among the evening's performances are: the Overture to Luisa Miller; *Kónya's "In fernem Land" (Lohengrin); Arroyo's "Tacea la notte placida"* (Il Trovatore); *Kirsten's "Depuis le jour"* (Louise); *Macurdy and chorus's "O Isis und Osiris"* (Die Zauberflöte); *Corena and Ezio Flagello's "Un segreto d'importanza"* (La Cenerentola). *Following the second intermission, the curtains part to reveal Bing and company in a farewell ceremonial (page 174; and pages 176–7). The breathtaking last moments belong to Birgit Nilsson (page 175), in the Final Scene from Strauss's* Salome.

A SUPPLEMENTARY GUIDE TO THE PHOTOGRAPHS

Many of the photographs in this book are group shots. The principal artists are discussed in the captions; this page-by-page guide to the photographs is intended as an aide-mémoire for the reader who will want to identify more singers and other well-known figures in the world of opera than those who are mentioned in the text. All identifications are from left to right.

PAGES

5, *bottom:* Renata Tebaldi, Giuseppe Campora
6, *upper left:* Gladys Swarthout
15, *left:* Perle Mesta (foreground)
16-17, *extreme right:* Elsa Maxwell
18, *bottom:* Ambassador and Mrs. Henry Cabot Lodge
24, *top:* Paul Franke (behind Rudolf Bing and Zachary Solov); *bottom center:* Cesare Valletti, Roberta Peters, Fernando Corena, Hertha Glaz
27, *upper left:* Ignace Strasfogel, Victoria de los Angeles, Frank Guarrera, Robert Herman
31, *lower left:* Francis Robinson; *bottom right:* Rudolf Bing (left)
46: (foreground) Bidú Sayão, (standing) Rudolf Bing, unidentified, G. Lauder Greenway, Anthony Bliss, unidentified, Giovanni Martinelli, John Brownlee (partially obscured), Wilfred Pelletier, (seated, at right) Mimi Benzell, Rose Bampton, Licia Albanese
53, *lower right:* (first row) Robert Herman, William Walker, William Weibel, Nathaniel Merrill, unidentified, Zinka Milanov, Anselmo Colzani, Louis Sgarro, Richard Tucker
54, *upper left:* Jean Morel, Kurt Adler; *upper right:* Helen Vanni, Evangeline DeFlorio, Emilia Cundari, James McCracken, Cyril Ritchard
55, *upper left:* Cyril Ritchard, a member of the corps de ballet, Mary Ellen Moylan, Zachary Solov; *upper right:* unidentified, James McCracken, Nathaniel Merrill, Kurt Adler, Cyril Ritchard, Maurice Valency, Jean Morel; *bottom:* Cyril Ritchard and Mary Ellen Moylan (seated), Geoffrey Holder (bowing)
57, *top:* (center, rear) Mattyln Gavers, Cyril Ritchard
58, *top:* Cesare Siepi, Gabriella Tucci, Roberta Peters; *bottom:* (foreground) Lisa Della Casa, Cesare Valletti, Eleanor Steber, Cesare Siepi
59, *right:* Cesare Valletti, Fernando Corena (rear), Cesare Siepi
60: Cesare Siepi
61, *top:* Cesare Siepi with members of the corps de ballet; *bottom:* Roberta Peters, Theodor Uppman
66, *top left:* Gladys Kriese, Elfego Esparza; *center left:* Teresa Stratas, Hermann Prey, Judith Raskin; *bottom left:* Hermann Prey, Lisa Della Casa
67, *top:* Teresa Stratas, Cesare Siepi, Judith Raskin; *bottom:* Gladys Kriese, Judith Raskin, Cesare Siepi, Elfego Esparza
82-3: (foreground) Nina Morgana, Ruth Miller, Charles Kullmann (partially obscured), Edith Mason, Stella Roman, Risë Stevens, Marjorie Lawrence, Elisabeth Rethberg, Martha Lipton, Alexander Kipnes (partially obscured), Lotte Lehmann, Raoul Jobin, Helen Jepson, Rudolf Bing (standing), Frederick Jagel, Richard Crooks, Nanette Guilford, Mario Chamlee (partially obscured), Hertha Glaz, Vilma Georgiou, John Brownlee (partially obscured)
88-9: (foreground) Robert Merrill, Regina Resnik, Roberta Peters, Judith Raskin, Blanche Thebom, Mary Curtis-Verna, Nicolai Gedda (partially obscured), Anna Moffo, Norman Scott (rear, partially obscured), Gabriella Tucci, Rosalind Elias, Clifford Harvuot, John Robert Dunlap, Osie Hawkins, Richard Tucker, Mildred Miller, Teresa Stratas, Mignon Dunn, Justino Diaz, Robert Schmoor, William Walker, Eleanor Steber, Lorenzo Alvary, Jean Madiera, Gerhard Pechner
101, *lower right:* Mrs. Rudolf Bing (second from left)
111, *top right:* Joan Sutherland and Richard Tucker; *second from top, right:* Corneil MacNeil, Rosalind Elias, Kurt Adler, Richard Tucker; *third from top, right:* Louis Sgarro, Joann Grillo, Richard Tucker, Francesco Molinari-Pradelli, Leontyne Price, Robert Merrill
112, *top:* Renata Tebaldi, Renata Scotto, Delia Rigal, Anna Moffo, Phyllis Curtin, Robert Merrill, Lowell Wadmond
113, *top:* (foreground) Rudolf Bing, Joan Sutherland, Robert Merrill, Gabriella Tucci, Renata Tebaldi, Renata Scotto
120, *lower left:* (foreground) Osie Hawkins, Lowell Wadmond, Dorothy Kirsten
124, *upper left:* Birgit Nilsson; *top right:* Jess Thomas
128-9: Loren Driscoll (center right), Benno Kusche (supine)
131, *bottom:* (right of center, foreground) Pilar Lorengar, Giorgio Tozzi
132, *center left:* Teresa Stratas, Fernando Corena, Teresa Zylis-Gara, Rosalind Elias; *bottom left:* Pietro Bottazzo, Tom Krause, Fernando Corena, Teresa Stratas, Teresa Zylis-Gara, Rosalind Elias
132-3, *center:* Teresa Zylis-Gara, Rosalind Elias
133, *right:* Rosalind Elias, Tom Krause

146, *top:* (left, foreground) Sándor Kónya, (right) Rod MacWherter, Edmond Karlsrud, Edith Mathis, Pilar Lorengar

149, *upper right:* Osie Hawkins, August Heckscher

164, *left:* Rudolf Bing; *upper right:* Robert Merrill, Cesare Siepi

165, *upper right:* Robert Merrill, Placido Domingo

166–7: (clockwise, from left) Elisabeth Waldheim, Nina Bing (partially obscured), Rafael Kubelik, Marit Gentele, U.N. Secretary-General Kurt Waldheim, Mary Lindsay, Rudolf Bing, Elsie Kubelik, Beatrice Gentele, Göran Gentele

173, *top:* Enrico Di Giuseppe, Lucine Amara, Cesare Siepi, Raymond Gniewek

174–5: Teresa Stratas, Enrico Di Giuseppe (partially obscured), Rosalind Elias, Richard Tucker, Sherrill Milnes (partially obscured), Göran Gentele, Edmond Karlsrud, George Moore (partially obscured), Rudolf Bing, Gabriella Tucci, Anna Moffo

176–7: (foreground) unidentified, Zachary Solov, Lucine Amara, Jon Vickers, Pilar Lorengar, Régine Crespin, Gail Robinson, Teresa Stratas, Rosalind Elias, Sherrill Milnes (rear), Richard Tucker, Edmond Karlsrud (rear, partially obscured), Göran Gentele, George Moore, Lowell Wadmond, Rudolf Bing, Anna Moffo, Placido Domingo, Grace Bumbry, Osie Hawkins, Dorothy Kirsten, Paul Plishka (rear, partially obscured), James Levine, Leontyne Price, Richard Best (rear), Leonie Rysanek, Irene Dalis, Loretta Di Franco, unidentified

DESIGN AND PRODUCTION NOTES

This book was set photographically by TypoGraphic Innovations, Inc. and TypoGraphics Communications, Inc., New York, N.Y. Printed by Halliday Lithograph Corp., West Hanover, Mass. and bound by H. Wolff Book Mfg. Co., New York, N.Y.

The text type, Helvetica Light, formerly called Neue Haas Grotesk, is a Swiss sans serif face designed by M. Miedinger. The display types are Snell Roundhand and Stymie Black.

Snell Roundhand, designed by Matthew Carter, is based on the hand of Charles Snell, an early English writing master. Stymie Black is based on the linotype face Memphis. Although a derivative face, Stymie is a more advanced style that reflects greater simplicity.

Book design by Ira Teichberg.